THE PATH TO MARRIAGE

THE PATH TO MARRIAGE

DARING TO SAY 'I WILL' THROUGH FAITH

MARKUS GRAULICH

and

RALPH WEIMANN

GRACEWING

Im Glauben das "Ja" wagen. Auf dem Weg zur Ehe
First published in 2015
by Herder: Freiburg/Basle/Vienna, 2015
English translation by Cyprian Blamires

First published in 2017 by
Gracewing
2 Southern Avenue
Leominster
Herefordshire HR6 0QF
United Kingdom
www.gracewing.co.uk

ISBN 978 085244 898 4

Typeset by Gracewing

Cover design by Bernardita Peña Hurtado

*DEDICATED TO COUPLES
WHO FOLLOW THE PATH
OF FAITH AND FAITHFULNESS*

CONTENTS

ABBREVIATIONS

AL =   Pope Francis, Apostolic Exhortation *Amoris laetitia*

CCC =   *Catechism of the Catholic Church*

CIC =   *Codex Iuris Canonici*, 1983

CSDC=   *Compendium of the Social Doctrine of the Church*

EV =   Pope John Paul II, Encyclical *Evangelium vitae*

FC =   Pope John Paul II, Apostolic Exhortation *Familiaris Consortio*

GS =   Second Vatican Council, *Gaudium et Spes*

HV =   Paul VI, Encyclical *Humanae vitae*

LF =   Pope Francis, Encyclical *Lumen fidei*

LS =   Pope Francis, Encyclical *Laudato si*

FOREWORD

Marriage is a real adventure, and there are different ways to talk about adventures. In the present work, the main emphasis is on those aspects which are most important if couples are to make a success of the adventure of marriage. It is intended to serve as *a Guide to Marriage* and as a *support to married couples*. It sets out the foundational elements of a Christian marriage, elements that are to be regarded not as limitations or as burdens, but as positive guidelines for a life lived happily as a joint enterprise. Nowadays, there is so much talk about marriage breakdown, but we are seldom told about how to avoid such breakdown and how to make a success of a life shared with a spouse. This is what the present work is about.

In calling the two Synods on the family, Pope Francis demonstrated his great awareness of how pressing the need is to give more attention to marriage and the family. The Synod Fathers called for a strengthening of families and the beauty of marriage and family life were repeatedly stressed in the Synod, whilst thanking families for their witness. In his concluding address in 2015, Pope Francis appealed to everyone to recognise that the institution of the family was based on the indissoluble bond between a man and a woman that provides a the foundation for society and for human life. In his Apostolic Exhortation *Amoris laetitia* he summed up the thoughts and suggestions of the Synod Fathers, offering them to the Church as a basis for further considerations.[1]

People need to be encouraged to dare to follow their path through life together. The Church sees herself in this context not in the role of an agency which 'knows better', but as a Mother and Teacher,[2] keeping lovingly close to individuals and aiming to help them to find the key to life in general and to married life in particular. Marriage preparation and accompaniment are part of this, for a lifetime commitment should not be a leap into the unknown, and can be made properly only on the basis of a free will and with mature reflection.

The present work emphasises those aspects of marriage that are most in need of serious thought, and it sets out to use practical questions as a stimulus to further reflection. These questions are directed at individuals in the first place, but they are also to be understood as opportunities for discussion by couples. The idea is to help both individuals preparing for marriage and married couples who have already said 'I will' to each other to make better sense of how to live their life together. There is no attempt to evade difficulties, and the focus is on shaping the kinds of attitudes that will make it possible for marriage to be less of an impossibly risky gamble and more of an ultimately happy and harmonious adventure. This book aims to offer recommendations as to how the marriage vows can be lived faithfully and successfully: When that happens, a precious witness is given to society at large. Our underlying conviction is that faith in God helps us to understand the essence of marriage and to accept the challenges presented by it.

Notes

1   See Pope Francis, Apostolic Exhortation *Amoris laetitia*.
2   Cf. Pope John XXIII, Encyclical *Mater et magistra*.

INTRODUCTION

The state of marriage today is in a difficult position. On the one hand the 'men and women of our postmodern world run the risk of rampant individualism'.[1] On the other hand they are faced with a huge variety of forms of cohabitation, all more or less enjoying social recognition. What we are witnessing today is the rise of a culture of non-commitment and disconnectedness, a culture which makes it more difficult for both State and Church marriage alike. Having witnessed marital disasters for themselves in their own families or circles of friends, many people are too frightened of permanent marital commitments to expose themselves to the same risk. Others again slide into marriage without ever having really made their own decision to marry. They emerge from the experience of more or less uncommitted cohabitation to continue their partnership as a marriage without having the least awareness that there is any difference between the two things.

Then there is the virtual world and the new challenges it presents. Much of social life today involves the social media, and therefore it is subjected to the laws of social communication 'which enable us to choose or eliminate relationships at whim, thus giving rise to a new type of contrived emotion which has more to do with devices and displays than with other people and with nature.'[2] This new reality fundamentally alters the process of entering into a relationship and interpersonal communication. When loving relationships are based on a foundation of Internet chat, Twitter, or similar such media, they are easily

> **Being in a real relationship and not in a virtual one**

subject to deception. In circumstances like these, individuals have a virtual rather than a real relationship. Although there may be an apparent closeness, real relationships only very occasionally develop between persons having 'a virtual connection', for this kind of connection simply does not have the capacity to replace a personal encounter.

In the sphere of social policy, and not least against the background of gender ideology,[3] the traditional model of marriage as a long-lasting commitment between a man and woman to a shared life is called into question. At the same time the attempt is being made to put it on the same level as forms of same-sex shared life or uncommitted forms of temporary cohabitation. Meanwhile successive experiences of failed cohabitations leave individuals with scars and wounds that inevitably intensify a sense of loneliness and mistrust.

Nonetheless, a new yearning for true and truthful relationships and for faithfulness and love can be detected among the youth and (young) adults. Life can be lived only once, and time spent never returns. The saying *Carpe Diem*, 'seize the day' of the Roman poet Horace has a new relevance.[4] To meet the needs of the hour; ideals, guidelines, and principles are called for that are not vulnerable to the accusation of being ideological. A good marriage is a really great treasure.

The Catholic Church has the task of making this treasure accessible to the people of today—and that means to everyone. The Catholic understanding of marriage as a sacrament of the faith is to be understood as an invitation to commit wholeheartedly to the option of a shared life. Far from leading into the depths of disaster, this option can be a way to happiness and fulfilment. Fleeting connections based on the postmodern axiom *anything goes* are replaced by the true

A true and truthful 'I love you' instead of fleeting liaisons

and truthful *I love you* of a life shared for good. The call of Jesus to an imperishable love that leads to an indissoluble marriage (Mt 19:6) amounts to the same thing.

Contemporary developments in society have then made marriage preparation and marriage accompaniment much more important than they used to be. This is not simply a matter of providing the kind of guidelines needed by those who take the risk of contracting a Catholic marriage: it is also about helping people to understand that the Church vision of marriage does not make excessive demands on people and remains perfectly appropriate even in today's world. In other words, the ideal of marriage can become a lived reality only when a man and a woman dare to say 'I will' in faith. As the Synod emphasised, the Church must encourage (young) persons to accept the riches that the sacrament of marriage can give them.[5] This sacramental bond consecrates the marriage union and makes it possible by the grace of the Holy Spirit for marriage to become a living sign of the union between Christ and His Church.[6]

Marriage in the Church is thus not simply a matter of having a beautiful external setting for the wedding; it actually confers an 'added value' on the marital union, in that through the sacrament of marriage which they receive before the sight of God, the spouses are 'strengthened and consecrated at the same time'[7] for their life together, and receive grace. They will still have to face the difficulties and everyday challenges that individuals encounter when they share the same home, but they will do so on the basis of a solid foundation that will enable them to overcome such difficulties. Indeed their mutual 'I will' is both enveloped in and carried by the eternal 'I will' of God to each partner.

Christian marriage builds on natural marriage: it was not originally constituted by Christ but raised by Him to a sacrament. In other words, the sacrament of marriage as contracted in the Church has its natural foundation in creation, in the complementarity of man and woman in their interdependence. The Catholic understanding of marriage rests on the foundation in creation, but the Church sets marriage in the context of faith and dependence on God's presence.

Faith gives us the key to a deeper understanding of the plan of God laid down in creation with respect to marriage; through faith that plan can bear fruit in individual marriages. This raises the question as to how those facing the decision of whether or not to get married can access this key. How can they know what marriage is according to God's plan in creation and according to the faith? How can faith make marriage fruitful, and how does faith help married couples to live out their union?

In the fast-paced postmodern world, the Church has the important task of proclaiming the eternally valid injunctions of Jesus Christ about marriage. In this way she serves both God and mankind, for in obedience to the command of God she gives us guidelines for making a success of life. Marriage is not something secondary, for—in the words of John Paul II—it is nothing less than the 'nucleus of society'. More work needs to be done in the area of the pastoral care of marriage, to show (young) people that a shared life can work out happily and that it is a source of fulfilment and self-realisation. They need to be helped not just to settle for what is merely transient, but to look for the lasting happiness which will give their life together security and fulfilment.

When a couple go up to the altar they are usually nervous and in all likelihood a little tense. They have so much on their minds. Therefore, it is a good thing, that the liturgical service has a clear structure, which gives them a sense of security and peace. But while the Church wedding ceremony provides the context, it is actually much more than that. For it involves the naming and confirming before God and the community of the elements that are really essential for marriage. Those elements need to be discussed and worked through beforehand in the marriage preparation course. So the chapters of this book refer to the rite of marriage, though without necessarily following it word for word. (The texts for the celebration of marriage can be found in the Appendix.) The aim is to provide the reader with a step-by-step guide to the essence of marriage from the standpoint of faith. But before we can consider the elements essential to marriage, we need to take a look at how Christian marriage is appropriate to our nature as human beings.

FOR FURTHER REFLECTION

- *Why have I decided I want to get married (in church)?*
- *What makes a relationship valuable for me?*
- *Has my faith got anything to do with this relationship?*
- *Can I really get deeply involved with another person, or do I just remain on the surface?*
- *Is there an ideal of marriage for me?*

Notes

1   LS 162.
2   *Ibid.* 47.
3   Cf. AL 56.
4   See Horace, *Odes* 1,11.
5   Cf. AL 40.
6   Cf. *ibid.* 11; 72.
7   GS 48.

1. WHAT IS MARRIAGE REALLY ABOUT?

The Evangelist reports that Pharisees came to Jesus 'who wanted to put a case to him and asked: "Is it against the Law for a man to divorce his wife on any pretext whatever?"' He answered:

> Have you not read that the Creator from the beginning made them male and female and that he said. This is why a man leaves his father and mother and becomes attached to his wife, and the two become one flesh? They are no longer two, therefore, but one flesh. So then, what God has united, human beings must not divide (Mt 19:3–6).

In this brief conversation between Jesus and the Pharisees, what He really wants to say in his preaching about marriage becomes clear. He does not simply confirm the practice of his time, which took for granted the possibility of divorce—just as it took for granted the prevalence of the arbitrary treatment of women by men. For Jesus there is much more to it: in his proclamation of the Kingdom of God he wants to emphasise the real purpose of God with regard to marriage.

Jesus contrasts 'the original'[1] with what 'is done' and what 'our ancestors' did, and he thereby renews our understanding of marriage as something related to creation. Matthew's Gospel emphasises this aspect, which is expressed in the words 'it was not like this from the beginning' (Mt 19:8). Man is made 'in the image of God',

Jesus contrasts 'the ancient' with 'the original'

like God (cf. Gn 1:26), and this reflects the greatness of human dignity, applying as it does to *every* person without distinction. Every person has this dignity, and no one can be deprived of it. It can be damaged, it can be denied him, but nothing and nobody can take it from him. Mutual respect for one another is always an expression of this dignity.

From this point of view, it is also clear that man is a being made for relationships. This aptitude for building relationships extends to almost all areas of life and includes our relationship with God, with a neighbour, and with the environment as well.

> God did not create man as a solitary being, 'for from the beginning male and female he created them' (Gn 1:27). Their companionship produces the primary form of interpersonal community. For by his innermost nature man is a social being, and unless he relates himself to others he can neither live nor develop his potential.[2]

Another important aspect is connected with the image-of-God-idea which gives the Christian picture of man its unchangeable character. God is described in the First Letter of John as Love *itself* (cf. 1 Jn 4:8). If God is love, then we may say that man created in the image of God is called to love. The Letter of John expresses this as follows: 'My dear friends, let us love one another, since love is from God and everyone who loves is a child of God and knows God.' (1 Jn 4:7) The calling to love is connected with the idea of creation: man is made for love and destined for love. 'Only through an encounter with God are we able to see in the other something more than just another creature, to recognise the divine image in the other, thus truly coming to discover him or her and to mature in a love that becomes concern and care for the other.'[3]

When he talks about marriage, Jesus **Marriage under-**
refers to this original understanding: he **stood and lived**
thus sets himself in opposition to the view **as a way of**
of marriage current in his day, which **discipleship**
allowed a man to dismiss a woman from
a marriage. In opposition to this practice, Jesus emphasises the
significance of the creation-based view, which tells us that
man is called to love and that the model for this love is God's
love. This has implications for our understanding of marriage:
it means that a wife is no longer to be subjected to the arbitrary
will of her husband, nor the husband to the arbitrary will of
the wife; rather, love is to be a long-term commitment. The
commandment to love God and neighbour thus finds concrete expression in marriage, and marriage can be understood
and lived as a way of discipleship.

In connecting the idea of marriage to creation, Jesus
opens our eyes in his teaching to the truth and beauty of
marriage as it was intended to be right from the very beginning. Jesus binds his understanding of marriage to the Creator. It is He whom one encounters in Jesus Christ who
discloses the full meaning of marriage as set forth at the
creation. The New Testament teaching about marriage takes
its character from Him. For 'Christ … by the revelation of
the mystery of the Father and His love, fully reveals man to
himself and makes his supreme calling clear.'[4] Paul emphasises this when he tells us that Christians have to contract
their marriages and live them 'in the Lord' (1 Co 7:39).

Just as in the Old Testament the prophets use the image
of marriage to describe the union of God with man, so the
New Testament connects the union of the married couple
with the relationship between Christ and His Church. The
logic underlying this is profound, as the author of the Letter
to the Ephesians tells us: 'This is why a man leaves his father
and mother and becomes attached to his wife, and the two

become one flesh. This mystery has great significance, but I am applying it to Christ and the Church' (Ep 5:31ff).

Marriage as understood in its creational meaning and marriage as understood in the light of faith belong together. In the Church, the mutual interrelationship of man and woman as founded in creation becomes a sacrament. So marriage becomes a sign of the union of God with man, of Christ with his Church.

This is expressed in the nuptial blessing as follows:

> *Holy Father,*
> *Who formed man in your own image,*
> *male and female you created them,*
> *so that as husband and wife, united in body and heart,*
> *they might fulfil their calling in the world;*
> *O God, who, to reveal the great design you formed in your love,*
> *willed that the love of spouses for each other*
> *should foreshadow the covenant you graciously made with your people,*
> *so that, by fulfilment of the sacramental sign, the mystical marriage of Christ with his Church might become manifest in the union of husband and wife among your faithful ...*

Down through the centuries, the Church has sought to proclaim in every culture the model of marriage founded in creation and renewed by Jesus, the model of marriage as a personal union of man and woman for the whole of life. This teaching has all too frequently encountered contradiction, rejection, and misunderstanding, just as was the case in the time of Jesus (cf. Mt 19:10).

In Ancient Rome, a stronghold of the multicultural and the multireligious practices, where adultery, divorce, homosexuality, injustice, evil and so forth (cf. Rm 1:22–32) were the order of the day, such a view of marriage was inevitably regarded as hopelessly demanding. And yet—not least through the lived witness of Christian married couples—

the beauty of Christian togetherness in marriage and family gradually found acceptance. Hence in Rome and elsewhere, the lived culture initially and then the legal order too was first of all influenced by the teaching of the Church about marriage as founded in the order of creation, and then subsequently brought into conformity with it.

In this light our society, which has long ceased to be homogeneously Christian, could be seen as similar to Ancient Rome, at least with regard to the divergence between the demands of the Bible and social reality. All the more urgent is it for the Christian understanding of marriage to be made accessible again. As Pope Francis emphasised in his address at the conclusion of the Synod on the Family in 2015, this can be achieved by the adoption of a joyful and confident pastoral approach capable of calming the anxieties felt by (young) people about taking irrevocable decisions. The real self-fulfilment, which many people are inclined to seek (all too often unsuccessfully) in all kinds of hazardous relationship scenarios actually becomes reality in Christian marriage. The marriage vows that the couple make to each other at their wedding are not then primarily about 'swimming against the tide'; rather, they encourage a reawakening of the original sense of marriage.

If the desired result is to be achieved, bride and groom need to be aware of the different elements of the promise they are making. They can then see what marriage is all about and what is involved in a partnership. They come to understand that the statements contained in the marriage vow correspond in the deepest possible way to the essence of the person and his dignity, which has its root in the fact of being-in-the-image-of-God. Faith will help them to breathe life into their marriage vows and to be faithful to them.

FOR FURTHER REFLECTION

- *Have I ever thought about the Biblical understanding of marriage?*
- *What does it mean to me that man is made in the image of God?*
- *How can Holy Scripture be a support for me in marriage?*
- *Do I see marriage as a calling and a way of discipleship?*

Notes

1   Joseph Ratzinger, 'Zur Theologie der Ehe' in *Theologische Quartal-schrift* 149 (1969), 54; now in *Joseph Ratzinger Gesammelte Schriften* 4, 567.

2   GS 12.

3   Pope Benedict XVI, Encyclical *Caritas in Veritate*, 11.

4   GS 22.

2. I DO TAKE THEE

T he words 'I do take thee' in the marriage vows have a huge significance—but they can no longer be taken for granted nowadays. For a variety of reasons, people in our society are less and less willing to commit to a permanent union. Along with the prevalence of individualism, another factor is that some people lack the capacity to accept themselves and indeed may actually be confused about themselves. In their insecurity, they identify with persons or with qualities that have nothing or little to do with the reality of their own lives. Instead of accepting the personality they actually have, they escape into a (virtual) apparent world and take on roles that are not really appropriate for them. And yet in truth it is actually the acceptance of oneself (nothing to do with egoism) that provides the basis for the acceptance of the other.

It is just this acceptance that needs to be assumed where marriage is concerned. The social trend is to reduce relationships between individuals to virtual and short-lived contacts, whereas Catholic marriage involves the making of a crucial vow that is real and enduring: 'I do take thee'. It is in this that married love finds its own particular expression.

When you take each other as man and wife, you are giving each other a home and receiving a home from each other. Each spouse can feel at ease in relationship, each spouse can experience security and find a place to be at home. More than ever, the 'world citizen' in a globalised world needs such a place where he/she

Accepting one another means giving and receiving home

can be at home, where he/she can experience safety[1] and
security.

When two people take each other, it gives them a real
help towards fulfilling that yearning which everyone experiences to find their niche in life, to be protected, to be
recognised, understood, and loved as a person, to experience
tenderness and nearness. The experience of being accepted
helps to enhance a spouse's dignity, it gives the individual
the key to self-discovery through union in freedom. This
personal mutual acceptance includes the sexual element, but
that will only be a part of it. For it is as much about
encouragement and hope for us in our longing for the
limitless and the absolute in time.

Accepting another person means committing to the risks
involved in a shared life, growing in dialogue with that
person, discovering and achieving one's fullest potential
together with that person. However, taking another person
is not tantamount to forming the kind of symbiotic relationship that first love may yearn for. Rather, it is about a
unity in togetherness that does not threaten the difference
and the individuality of the other. Love in marriage 'does
not mean self-abandonment and the quest for a perfect
fusion in an impossible 'unity'. *Love always involves two
persons*, there is no love without someone who is the object[2]
of that love, someone who is facing[3] me. Pure love is
possible only from person to person: it involves distance in
harmony, reverence, giving space to the otherness of the
other and letting the other be.'[4]

The charm of togetherness derives from just this difference (though there does of course at the same time need to
be agreement in regard to the foundational issues of a
shared life). The couple broaden each other's horizons,
challenge each other, and love each other. The person
always remains something of a 'mystery', he never makes

himself fully known, his self is inevitably subject to change and exposed to a wide range of different influences. This means that self-acceptance and self-giving on the part of the marriage partners remains a continuing task. 'It is better to give than to receive', as the popular saying goes. While egoism blocks us up, true love gives itself and accepts others.

This is the way for the individual to overcome his preoccupation with himself and take the other for the other's sake. In doing so, he opens **"I do take** himself up to the other and thereby moves **thee" means:** outside the circle around himself and out- **making space** side his existing family connections (cf. Gn **for something** 2:24), which makes it possible for a new **new to grow** family unit to arise. In this context, difference and oneness are not seen as opposites, but experienced as a source of potential. 'I do take thee' leads to the creation of a space between the two persons where something new can emerge and grow.

Acceptance is the key to the 'I will' said to the spouse and this 'I will' is to be understood as all-em- **Acceptance** bracing. It signals a readiness to accept the **means** other person unconditionally, including **keeping in** that person's past, present, and future. The **touch with the** spouses can have only the sketchiest notion **reality of your** of what lies before them in the future or of **spouse** what they are to expect from marriage, but their everyday experience of marriage may be very strongly marked by the experiences that each of them brings to it. These can have a positive effect on their life together but they may also be burdensome. Thus acceptance of each other entails an openness to each other and a sharing of experiences. Remaining silent about these out of a misplaced fearfulness can cause problems not just for each spouse individually but also for the marital relationship as such. It is important then to clear the decks before marrying. When significant facts go unmentioned (for example if one is sterile, or if one has had a child by a previous relationship, or been in prison, or had a serious illness, and so forth), this is not simply a matter of a lack of openness, it must actually be understood as deception, a deception which can damage the marriage or which could even lead to its nullity.

Acceptance means that I keep in touch with the reality of my spouse. An attitude like this requires selflessness but it gifts the spouse with security and trust, meaning that we can count on each other unconditionally.

The theme of acceptance represents a more difficult challenge in a society which has come under the influence of Gender Ideology. Whom or what can one really accept, and where are the boundaries of love to be placed? Is everything that may be regarded as possible also to be considered good, purely for the sake of not exposing oneself to the accusation of discriminating against someone? How far does man create himself and his environment; and how far can he go in regard to the concrete shaping of his own life?

In March 2015, the case of a 31-year old London woman caused a sensation: she claimed that she was in love with a tree and wanted to marry it. Many similar examples could be mentioned, and they reflect the fundamental problem of postmodernity, which assumes that doing one's own thing is the ideal to be followed. In this view, acceptance matters much less than that we actively choose and construct what we are. A mentality like this not only damages the individuals who cannot accept themselves, but also impoverishes their relationships or indeed makes relationships impossible for them. Romano Guardini discussed this issue and saw in it the original sin of humanity. For in the time of testing, the first humans refused to accept themselves, wanting to be what they could not be.[5] Every time this happens, the stability of the given order of things is weakened and the relationship network is seriously disrupted.

Pope Francis has also alluded to this whole issue with reference to Guardini. Humans are predetermined as woman or man; they cannot embrace a new sexual identity for themselves but must accept what they are. Each person must respect the 'ecology of the human'. The nature of the human cannot be manipulated at will. So the important thing is to accept one's own body as a gift from God and to value one's own femininity or masculinity, an essential element in the encounter with the opposite sex. 'It is not a healthy attitude which would seek "to cancel out sexual difference because it no longer knows how to confront it"'.[6]

The Compendium of the Social Teaching of the Catholic Church strongly emphasises this principle, in opposition to the theses of so-called Gender Studies. Hence we have this statement: '*Everyone, man and woman, should acknowledge and accept his sexual identity.* Physical, moral, and spiritual *difference* and *complementarities* are oriented towards the goods of marriage and the flourishing of family life.'[7]

Acknowledgement of the other therefore assumes that I accept myself as I am, not as what I can or may want to be. This assumption is absolutely basic if the mutual reference of the sexes to one another is to become clear, as expressed in the creation story in the astonished cry: 'This one at last is bone of my bones and flesh of my flesh!' (Gn 2:23). The individual is not self-sufficient. On the contrary, the creation account makes it clear 'that man, who is the only creature on earth which God willed for itself, cannot fully find himself except through a sincere gift of himself'.[8]

At the same time this realism points to a contradiction in which parts of society find themselves. For there is a false conception of freedom, 'which exalts the isolated individual in an absolute way, and gives no place to solidarity, to openness to others and service of them'.[9] The promise 'I do take thee' constitutes a renunciation of the kind of individualism which takes any relationship down a one-way street. It is a renunciation of the technological mentality that treats everything as a question of planning and feasibility. By contrast it involves an assent—perhaps the most significant assent that any individual can in general give—acceptance of the other unconditionally and for his own sake and a willingness to throw in one's lot with the other on the journey of life.

FOR FURTHER REFLECTION

- *Have I faced up to my strengths and weaknesses and accepted them?*
- *Can I cope with myself, and where do I see the need to change myself?*
- *Am I hiding something from my partner? Are there things that 'have not been worked through'?*
- *What am I looking for in my spouse?*
- *Can I come to terms with his/her strengths and weaknesses?*

Notes

1 In the German the expression is *Geborgenheit.*
2 In the German the expression is *Gegenstand.*
3 In the German the expression is *gegenüber.*
4 Ida Friederike Görres, *Von Ehe und von Einsamkeit. Ein Beitrag in Briefen*, Vienna, 2012, 40–1.
5 Cf. Romano Guardini, *Die Annahme seiner selbst. Den Menschen erkennt nur, wer von Gott weiss*, Kevelaer, 2008, 31.
6 LS 155.
7 CSDC 224.
8 GS 24.
9 EV 19.

3. OF MY OWN FREE WILL AND CHOICE AND WITHOUT COMPULSION

The kind of acceptance of self and acceptance of the other that can found a lasting relationship does not develop overnight. Hence the celebrant asks the couple at the wedding service: 'Are you ready freely and without reservation to give yourselves to each other in marriage?'. To this the bride and bridegroom answer with a simple but meaningful 'I am'. They thereby confirm their readiness for marriage, which the Second Vatican Council defined as 'the intimate partnership of married life and love, … established by the Creator and qualified by His laws', and as 'rooted in the conjugal covenant of irrevocable personal consent'.[1]

It is in the nature of the marriage bond between man and wife to be a whole-life partnership. So marriage cannot be entered into without any preparation or on the basis of pure emotion. Taking a person in marriage for that person's own sake, promising that person lifelong faithfulness, love, respect, and reverence, are acts that must arise from a decision that is both mature and shared.

In other words, the marriage partners *must* know what they are doing. This can happen however only if the 'Yes' of the partners comes out of an inner freedom and in full awareness of the significance of their **Married couples must know what they are doing** decision. 'Love cannot be forced and it reveals itself precisely through its non-receptivity to any external pressure that runs contrary to the essence of marriage.'[2]

In today's world individuals have more freedom than ever: freedom from social pressures, from social guidelines and expectations, from strict norms for everyday behaviour and social life. Possible options seem to be endless, and they are placed before children and young persons from their earliest days. But this makes decisions all the more difficult. If everything is seen as permitted, possible, and equal in value, this raises the question: is everything actually good and can everything help us to make a success of life? Decisions about one's way of life have to be weighed carefully and thought through, for they will decide the future course of one's whole life.

The decision to get married must not therefore rest or be taken on the basis of superficial considerations, for the purpose of attaining other ends such as getting away from your parents for example, or escaping from an uncomfortable situation. Thus the Second Vatican Council stressed the significance of the free personal act 'whereby the spouses mutually bestow and accept each other'.[3] Freedom means both freedom in our being and freedom in our choosing, freedom *from* and freedom *for*. Freedom makes it possible for us to choose marriage—both on the purely human level and in the sense of a sacrament—for its own sake.

This freedom may be limited or excluded by various circumstances. A person who decides to get married while suffering from the death of a close relative, or who has not yet worked through the consequences of a tragic event in his own life, will make his decision in the thick of great emotional pressures and not in freedom. The same applies when at the time of the decision a person is suffering under some form of dependency—in the worst case ocenario this could amount to a full scale addiction. Today there is a widespread dependency on the Internet, and that not only limits a person's freedom but hinders interpersonal relationships just as much as dependency on drugs or alcohol.

Nor can a free decision be taken if the couple are influenced by fear or by external coercive pressures. The social pressure to marry that was exerted because couples were expecting a child has more or less disappeared, yet other forms of coercion and fear are often operative, sometimes emanating from one part of the couple. A free decision is not possible where for example one of the couple threatens suicide if the other refuses marriage, or where one of the couple exerts financial pressure or plays on the anxieties of the other.

It has been a great merit of the Church with respect to marriage that from the beginning she has emphasised and reinforced the principle that marriage must be based on a free choice on the part of the partners. It is not up to parents or families **Reinforcing the freedom of the partners** to decide about the marriage of their children. The partners themselves freely choose each other and choose to marry and say 'Yes' to each other. 'Freedom is learnt in the context of an actual attachment as a person takes on responsibility, stands on his own two feet, and in doing so opens up completely new perspectives.'[4]

When two persons bestow themselves to one another and each takes the other by an act of free will and thus commits to the sacrament of marriage, they are however taking a step which necessarily assumes the presence not just of freedom but also of a human, psychological, and spiritual maturity. The spouses achieve human maturity if they have solid qualities of character which make a shared life possible. They need to have fundamental values and virtues which can become guidelines for their own behaviour and form qualities of character. The cardinal virtues of prudence, justice, fortitude, and temperance, have the same long-lasting importance in this connection as the Christian virtues—obedience to the Ten Commandments and the theological virtues of faith, hope, and love.

In today's society the word 'virtuous' is hardly common currency, but the truth is that a shared life cannot work unless the spouses grow mature in the virtues. The proper exercise of freedom requires that the individual have the appropriate fundamental attitudes and basic commitments, virtues, and values; these need to have matured in the course of his life and conditioned his behaviour. It is primarily against this background that the kind of life can develop which makes it possible for individual decisions to be taken responsibly.

A remarkable little story may make this point easier to understand. A couple were going through severe problems in their marriage, the spouses had long since drifted apart and high walls had grown up between them. Everyone was suffering, and the couple were in danger of splitting up. They were for ever either shouting at each other or ignoring each other and their relationship was damaged to the core. In his despair, the husband looked deep into himself and recognised that he could not change his wife, or at least not as things stood. On the other hand, he recognised that he was perfectly well able to change himself. With this in mind he returned home after a business trip and asked his wife the next morning how he could make the day more pleasant for her. Her response was to get him to do various menial cleaning jobs, to show him how little he meant to her. He stuck to the biblical principle according to which evil can only be defeated by good (cf. Rm 12:21). Several weeks passed and the husband stayed faithful to his virtuous decision in the teeth of numerous humiliations. Gradually the walls between them began to crumble, as the wife recognised that she too had the capacity to change herself—and the marriage was saved.

As this story shows, psychological maturity is also part of marriage. When individuals decide to get married, it is important that they themselves have a stable personality, that they know themselves, and that they are close to their spouse. In the absence of these basics, it becomes almost impossible to live the married state. Respect, reverence, and love can only be accorded by a psychologically balanced and stable character.

There is something else important to be learnt from this story. The husband could only come to his decision 'to change himself' after he had first looked within himself and had a conversation with God. It was after he found his way back to God again that he could draw the strength from his relationship with God to make the first step. But this too requires spiritual maturity. The marital bond is based not just on emotions or friendship, it is much more about 'becoming one', and it involves the whole person, one's own and that of one's spouse. The person who is spiritually mature is sensitive to the demands of married life and capable of finding solutions in times of crisis. He is not driven by the mood of the moment and he possesses the requisite patience in his own behaviour and in his dealings with his spouse. The marriage bond is not simply about the physical dimension but includes the spiritual too, and this finds expression (among other ways) in the joint quest of the married couple for a deeper meaning in life—which is to be found in God.

Such maturity is (as St John Paul II affirmed) not to be confused with perfection. It is much more a question of possessing the necessary prerequisites for the success of a marriage. This kind of maturity cannot coexist with the kind of psychological distur-

Maturity is not to be confused with perfection

bances or sicknesses which make it impossible for a marriage to be lived as the intimate partnership of a whole life. The same is the case if one of the partners is limited by dependencies not only in his freedom but in his capacity to be faithful to his marriage vows.

One of these limitations can be a too-close relationship with parents. It is not at all unusual for there to be no proper letting go of the parental home, with parents exerting a strong influence on the new relationship. This means that freedom can be hindered and the decision to marry can be influenced in a negative way. There is a good reason why it says in the Holy Scripture 'That is why a man leaves his father and mother and becomes attached to his wife, and the two become one flesh' (Mt 19:5; cf. Gn 2:24). Something new begins with a marriage. Strengthened by the power of grace, the married couple will experience highs and lows on their shared journey. They can cope with these together as long as their decision to marry has been made freely and with the requisite maturity.

In this connection there is a further point to be considered, one that is often overlooked. In wide swathes of our society, people have become accustomed to cohabiting before marriage. The idea is that this is the way for them to 'mature' and find out whether they really get on with each other. Justifications like this are often put forward that are in reality based on muddled thinking—though we cannot explore the subject in depth here. The point is that this getting-used-to-each-other can in fact all too easily mean that instead of getting married on the basis of mature reflection and a commitment freely made, people tend to 'slide' into it.

The decision to marry often comes at the precise moment when the cohabitation is no longer experienced as fulfilling. The individuals concerned promise themselves that marriage will give them the stimulus they need. Sometimes a child may be on the way or hoped for, and a (Church) wedding may be desired.

What is fundamentally lacking in these cases is the kind of healthy detachment which would allow the persons concerned freely to make a choice, for the partners have grown used to each other by living together without having actually committed to each other. Various sociologists have pointed out the danger inherent in this.⁵ The conditions and relationships (the shared home, the shared bedroom, 'living together') that are involved in such a manner of life bind persons to each other in a way that prevents them from committing on the basis of mature and unpressured reflection. For precisely that reason, when partners in this situation want to get married, they were and are advised to live celibate and apart for a while before the planned wedding. This allows them both to commit freely on the basis of mature reflection. It also demonstrates that something new is beginning.

Ideas like these are unpopular and out of step with the spirit of the age. But they do give us food for thought, as the following story shows. A catechesis about marriage stirred up a lively debate, chiefly because the parents of the pupils taking part could not identify with the picture of marriage that was being painted. The priest could make no headway with his arguments, no matter how hard he tried. But then a woman stood up and said courageously in front of everybody that she and her spouse had not had sex before their marriage. A sudden silence fell on the room, a taboo seemed to have been broken. Then the woman added by way of clarification that this continence had helped her a great deal in coming to the free and conscious decision to marry her husband. She said that it had helped the two of them to get to know each other, and she compared her experience with our experience of light. Sexual enjoyment is a very bright light, one that all too easily obscures the other weaker lights that we also need to be aware of. Her choice had made it possible for her to become aware of these smaller lights and to elaborate on them. When the 'great light' was switched on after the wedding, it did not obscure the other lights but actually enhanced their brightness. The priest did not need to add anything to this, everyone found these words deeply moving.

Finally, a mature decision to get married also requires some considerations about the rights and duties involved in marriage. The Church assumes that the partners are in a position to commit to the responsibilities that marriage entails. At a time when young men often lack patterns for a happy married life and when developments in society go against the Christian view of marriage, it is especially important to assist young persons and young adults to become mature enough for marriage, beginning with the strengthening of their capacity for lasting, mature, and freely-made commitments and especially the commitment to an indissoluble union.

FOR FURTHER REFLECTION

- *What does the marriage covenant mean for me?*
- *What reasons do I have to propose marriage or to accept the proposal to get married?*
- *How free am I in my decision?*
- *What do I think of myself? Do I have a 'mature' personality?*
- *What kind of assumptions do I make about living with another person (virtues—values)?*
- *Have I really thought through my decision to get married, or was it just made on the spur of the moment?*

Notes

1   GS 48.
2   Dietmar Kretz, *Freiheit und Liebe. Eine Studie zum Ehesakrament,* Würzburg 2011, 81.
3   GS 48.
4   Kretz, *Freiheit und Liebe,* 84.
5   Cf. Scott M Stanley, e.g., *Sliding versus deciding: Inertia and the Premarital Cohabitation Effect,* in: *Family Relations* 55 (2006), 499–509.

4. BEFORE GOD

To choose to have a Catholic wedding means to give your life a very particular orientation. Your journey through life is now to be shared with another person, and the two of you want to support and help each other. In order to make this happen, you both promise at the altar to cement your union 'before God'. This phrase is not some kind of 'optional extra'—like an addition to an oath ('as God is my help')—which could even be omitted. It is not uncommonly viewed in this way, and people often see the words as a kind of formula that goes with the package of a church wedding. But the phrase is very far from being an 'optional extra', indeed it is a crucial element in the marriage contract, though it is often neglected—and that neglect is not infrequently at the root of the collapse of marriages.

The decision to get married before God means a decision by the couple to follow their path through life together with God. This says something very real about marriage, something crucial for its orientation. A Christian marriage never involves 'just' the two spouses, for they **Following your path together with God** always marry before God and with God. This is clear from the biblical image of marriage, which tells us that marriage is to be understood as a sign of the covenant of God with man and that its orientation towards God is a lifetime affair.

The biblical view of marriage is very demanding, for the married couple take as their ideal the love and faithfulness of God and the self-giving of Christ. Ida Friederike Görres pointed this out to a friend of hers who, preparing for her wedding, was tormented by doubts about her decision to marry, and put the Christian view to her in this way:

> Christian love calls not just for a great deal; it calls for *everything*. It generally only works where willingness is total: where one wants from the other—and offers to the other—not only a home, a child, physical fulfilment, support and counsel, while also wanting to keep his own life to himself. Where you agree about marital duties and rights [...] and in other things steer clear of your personal egoism. Marriage is not my life and your life but *our* life, something new.[1]

So the Christian picture of marriage is above all a realistic one: there is no idealistic vision of the spouse, he is seen as he is, with all his faults and weaknesses. It's not a matter of making very heavy demands on the spouse or expecting everything from him whether possible or not. The wrong kind of 'love' actually has a blinding effect, and sooner or later the realities of life—including one's own faults, weaknesses, and difficulties—will catch up with a relationship based on that.

It is precisely because of these limits, which mean that the perfect partner does not exist, that it is essential to bring God into play. When God comes into the relationship, His presence can be the foundation for compensation and can give that fulfilment which the spouses are often not capable of providing by their own strength. This reduces tensions in the marriage and protects the couple from making excessive demands. In getting married before God, they recognise their love as a gift from God and place their future life under His blessing. They do not have to be God to each other, they do not have to guarantee eternal fulfilment to each other. But they should and will stay close to God on their journey. They entrust themselves to His accompanying care, and then He is able to give their love permanence and fulfilment

When spouses live before God, when they make God a part of their relationship, then—witness innumerable successful marriages—the way they enter into their relationship changes. They understand each other as gift from God and accept one another on that basis. They look at their spouse and at his life story, his strengths and weaknesses, from the perspective of faith. They see in the other a spouse created in the image of God and a spouse loved by Him. In this way respect and forgiveness, reverence and love, trust and devotion, humility and goodness—along with many other aspects of a shared life—will really begin to become possible, and the couple will find themselves undergoing a reorientation.

For this to happen however, God must not remain a 'stranger' in the relationship, he must be an essential part of it. This becomes clearly defined in the fact that the couple prays together—which establishes a kind of seismograph for the 'relationship of three'. The spouses may well not be at ease initially with the idea of praying together, but where this is practised it opens up a gushing spring from which flows the strength for a shared life, a readiness to forgive, positive change, mutual growth, faithfulness, and true love.

An illustration of how this can work out in practice can be found in the Old Testament Book of Tobit. Before the young married couple Tobias and Sarah come together, they turn to God in prayer:

> The parents meanwhile had gone out and shut the door behind them. Tobias rose from the bed and said to Sarah, 'Get up, my sister! You and I must pray and petition our Lord to win his grace and protection.' She stood up, and they began praying for protection, and this was how he began:
> 'You are blessed, O God of our fathers;
> blessed too is your name
> for ever and ever' (Tb 8:4–5).

When they prayed together it released such power that the force of evil, which had previously been all too real in the life of Sarah, could no longer harm the couple; now the blessing of God rested on them.

Unfortunately, the impression has arisen that prayer is to be understood in a purely individualistic way, so couples often find it difficult to pray together. Apart perhaps from grace before meals, praying together represents a big challenge for many, and initially it requires a considerable effort, but those who persist are rewarded. Praying morning and evening prayer together taps into a great source of power which strengthens the inner togetherness of marriage. A wise old saying goes that 'those who pray together stay together', they grow together and cope with problems together.

One of the reasons why a shared prayer life can be very difficult has to do with the omnipresence of the Media. Many couples spend their evenings in front of the television or the Internet, not unusually even in the bedroom. This does nothing to encourage them either to talk to each other or to pray with each other. Aside from the fact that these activities can be very damaging for the relationship, since the virtual world can never replace the real world, it becomes all the more difficult for them to make the effort needed to converse or to pray together.

Praying with one another and for one another Prayer together in marriage is about praying both with one another and for one another. That is how the journey on which the couple embark together becomes a spiritual journey and they become one in spirit. The prayer of Sarah and Tobias can serve as a pattern here, for in their prayer each one thanks God for the gift of the other and at the same time prays for the well-being of the other.

Thus praying together leads 'the life of the couple back to the divine spring, from which their being and all tenderness flow, and educates them to be authentic, capable of true giving, true welcome, and true sharing.'[2] For the married couple, praying together is the first building block if the marriage is to find stability and direction and a domestic church is to be created.

It is in prayer that faith shows itself, and faith is the response of man to God.[3] 'Believing in God means believing that there is no difficult situation that cannot be overcome. Faith is a source of added value for the couple, it makes them aware that they are not alone, so they become willing to follow the path to the end, no matter how long it may be.'[4] God invites the couple to follow their path together with Him, and it is through faith that they respond to this invitation.

In practice this can work out in different ways. A couple had a quarrel which was threatening to escalate. Having persisted with it even in front of the children, the parents both left the house for a time. Without any prior agreement on the matter, they each went to a different church to pray. When they got back home, they were able to forgive each other and throw themselves into each other's arms. They had found strength for this 'before God'.

From this point of view it is perfectly fitting to speak of marriage as a calling, for the married couple are called to make their journey before God and with God. The shared life of man and woman in which two persons give themselves to each other and take each other thus becomes a reflection of the divine love, which enriches that shared life of man and woman, perfects it, and brings it to fulfilment. Thus there are not a few couples able to say after 40 or 50 years of marriage that they are now living the most beautiful time of their lives together, for they have matured in their love and their love has with God's help and accompaniment found a deeper fulfilment.

To marry in the sight of God means, finally, to receive a sacrament. Sacraments are effective signs instituted by Christ of an invisible and real presence of His grace. In other words, something greater is involved under the outward action—an action which in this case is the celebration of the marriage at the altar in church. The Lord Himself is present at the celebration of a marriage, He blesses and hallows the union. Assuming the assent of the couple and their willingness to live their lives in the appropriate manner, He wants to walk the path together with them for ever. With this divine support (grace) to uphold them, their life together will bear fruit not only in the shape of children but also in the form of personal development, and this fruit will also be for the good of their fellows.

To live marriage as a sacrament means to recognise the primacy of God and to accept the graces the Lord wants to bestow on the union. The following statement by the Second Vatican Council is to be understood in just this way: 'For this reason Christian spouses have a special sacrament by which they are fortified and receive a kind of consecration in the duties and dignity of their state.'[5]

Committing to the calling to marriage in the sight of God means becoming aware of the huge significance of this commitment, which must on no account be made lightly or hastily. The knowledge that God is involved is comforting, it means that this far-reaching decision is to be pondered not simply by the couple on their own but also before God, in trust that God, who calls two persons to marriage, will help them to live the vows that they make to each other.

On the other hand, this shared foundation also provides those who are taking the risk of a commitment to marriage with a certain security. In today's society many people find it increasingly difficult to make lifetime commitments, so they get for ever postponed. In Italy men and women in their forties are still labeled 'young', which shows how widespread this mentality is. But if the human and spiritual elements are in place, people can surely take the plunge and marry earlier.

Another aspect of the question is significant in this respect. The community and the Church have the important task of helping (young) persons who get married to discover the beauty of Christian marriage. This will become all the more important, given the increasing social trend of turning against the ideal of a lasting marriage between man and woman. The fewer the models of successful lifelong partnership are experienced by young people in their own families and in their milieu, the harder it will be for them to opt for a Christian marriage. Therefore, preparation for marriage becomes all the more significant. As the Synod Fathers emphasise, this preparation is bound up with the invitation to the person concerned to practise his own faith consciously and committedly, in order to be able to live marriage and family as a calling. To this end, a marriage catechumenate is to be recommended as a method of shared preparation for married life and family life.[6]

A distinction is usually made between long-term preparation for marriage and the marriage preparation course as such; but both of these serve to develop an appreciation of marriage for what it is: a great gift. The long-term preparation, which begins as part of faith education in the family, consists in helping to identify and form those human and spiritual foundations which are necessary if couples are to make a success of their life together. This involves formation of character, of virtues and values, of a prayer life, of responsible attitudes, of an understanding of faithfulness and love and so forth. A person's understanding is brought in this way to maturity and his readiness for commitment along with it. The marriage preparation course itself, on the other hand, deals with the particular paths of individual couples towards their weddings.

Meanwhile a kind of 'marriage-follow-up' or marriage accompaniment is sometimes offered, for example with priests meeting up with couples every year, encouraging them to renew their marriage vows aiming to resolve problems where necessary, and generally offering support to couples on their journey together. In some parishes 'family apostolates' are established with the aim of supporting couples before and during their marriages. With this in mind the Synod suggested that 'Marriage and Family' issues be explored through catechesis, and it also pointed out the need for a special closeness to couples in times of crises and difficulties.[7] Initiatives like this are much to be recommended, for they mean that couples know they are not alone, they know that they are held together and carried by the great family of the Church. Thus each family is called to take its part in the mission of the Church.[8]

FOR FURTHER REFLECTION

- *Who is God for me?*
- *What role does God play in my life?*
- *What does God have to do with my relationship/marriage?*
- *Can I talk to my partner about God?*
- *Can I pray, how do I (we together) pray?*
- *What role do prayer and worship play in my/our life?*

Notes

1 Görres, *Von Ehe und von Einsamkeit*, 40.
2 Carlo Rochetta, 'Crisis in a Couple—How can one salvage a Relationship?', in: Aldegonde Brenninkmeijer-Werhahn, Klaus Demmer (eds.), *Close to our Hearts. Personal Reflections on Marriage*, Vienna/Berlin, 2013, 123.
3 Cf. LF 39.
4 Rochetta, 'Crisis in a Couple', 122.
5 GS 48.
6 Cf. Final Report of the Synod of Bishops, XIV Ordinary General Assembly, 57–58.
7 Cf. *ibid.*, 81; AL 255.
8 Cf. AL 281.

5. I WILL LOVE, HONOUR AND CHERISH YOU

hristian marriage is founded on a personal agreement that is described as follows in the Pastoral Constitution of the Second Vatican Council 'On the Church in the modern world': 'The intimate partnership of married life and love has been established by the Creator and qualified by His laws, and is rooted in the conjugal covenant of irrevocable personal consent. Hence by that human act whereby spouses mutually bestow and accept each other a relationship arises which by divine will and in the eyes of society too is a lasting one.'[1]

So where marriage is concerned we are not talking purely about a kind of 'contract', in which rights and duties are defined and conveyed, as with the purchase of a car. What marriage actually is and what rights and duties it involves cannot itself be made the object of a decision by the spouses, since it is a given. With marriage, we are talking about a qualitatively different relationship, one that has the person at the centre, for marriage is a *personal* union between man and woman. The married state brings with it a 'new quality' insofar as it takes as its model the covenant of God with humanity, and it is characterised by the mutual self-giving and receiving of the couple. This covenant and gift quality of marriage is clearly expressed in the wedding ceremony when the spouses say to each other: "I will have and hold you from this day forth, for better or worse, for richer or

poorer, in sickness and in health, to love and to cherish, till
death do us part."

Love excludes any kind of control, oppression or exploitation Love for one another, respect and honour for one another exclude *a priori* any form of control, oppression, or exploitation of the spouse. The spouse will not be seen as an object but as a subject. Love looks not first and foremost to the qualities, the talents, or the outward appearance of the spouse, but is oriented to the happiness and fulfilment of the other and finds therein its own fulfilment. This assumes that each spouse respects the other together with his history and dignity, and is also ready to see difference as enrichment and to embark together with the other on the path to human and spiritual growth.

'Thus a man and a woman, who by their compact of conjugal love "are no longer two, but one flesh" (Mt 19:6), render mutual help and service to each other through an intimate union of their persons and of their actions. Through this union they experience the meaning of their oneness and attain to it with growing perfection day by day'.[2] To this end a culture of conversation between the couple is necessary, a culture of mutual attentiveness, of mutual respect, of forgiveness and a genuine readiness to stand by one's spouse in the changes and chances of life. It is in the context of a life of sharing and cooperation like this that lived sexuality will become the language of love.

This language of love actually represents the most intensive form of communication between man and woman. It will however only prove to be a truthful language when the person-centred perspective is not neglected and the other is seen not as an object for satisfaction but as a loved person. As a result of an overemphasis on the erotic, sexuality has lost a great deal of its dignity and power. The exploitation of sexuality through pornography has played a huge part in turning it from a form of communication between man and woman into a way of living out desire and passion. The sexualisation of society and the ease of access to pornography just by a click on the Internet causes long-term damage to relationships. It degrades the human person and it also brings into marital intimacy pictures and ideas that have a destructive effect. The language of love falls silent when the quest for satisfaction wins the upper hand.

For the truth is that passion is as hard as the Underworld, a point emphasised in the *Song of Songs* (Sg 8:6). Passion has a hugely destructive potential, for its tendency is to take possession of the person—who then makes use of the other. Unfortunately, this turns sexuality, as the most intensive form of communication between the partners, into an untruthful language and in the long term into a lie. As the *Compendium of the Social Teaching of the Catholic Church* points out:

> In a society that tends more and more to relativise and trivialise the very experience of love and sexuality, exalting its fleeting aspects and obscuring its fundamental values, it is more urgent than ever to proclaim and bear witness that *the truth* of conjugal love and sexuality exists where there is a full and total gift of persons, with the characteristics of *unity* and *fidelity*.[3]

For sexuality to become the language of love, the person must be seen as a whole. It is of the essence of human personhood that the body has a language, a language expressed in nearness, security, warmth, tenderness, desire, and so forth. It must not be separated from the relationship of the spouses, for it belongs in this relationship, to the enrichment and fulfilment of which it contributes. Pope John Paul II affirmed that sexuality is fulfilled in truly human fashion only 'if it is an integral part of the love by

which a man and a woman commit themselves totally to
one another until death. The total physical self-giving
would be a lie if it were not the sign and fruit of a total
personal self-giving, in which the whole person, including
the temporal dimension, is present.'[4]

To avoid misunderstandings, we need to point out that
Christianity is not at all hostile to the body; its concern is
with the quality of the relationship between the couple.
Passionate love (*eros*) and selfless love (*agape*) belong insep-
arably together. Pope Benedict XVI developed this theme
in his Encyclical *Deus Caritas Est*, where he observed that
in marriage, body and soul should enter an inner union and
the challenge to this through Eros is to be accepted. A
glorification of the body in which sex is degraded to the
level of a commodity bought and sold, given and taken,
would turn the person himself into a commodity and love
into a caricature.[5] There is a pressing need to rediscover the
true dignity of the language of love in its different dimensions, and to understand it as the communication of love.

We need therefore to develop a comprehensive linguistic
culture in marriage, a culture which remains truthful both
in its verbal and in its non-verbal forms while also being
fully aware of the necessity of times of silence and of their
creative power. With regard to sexual activity as a language
of love, this silence is expressed in the exercise of marital
continence. There are moments in a marriage when the
expression of sexuality does not correspond to the reality of
the relationship. Problems and difficulties must be discussed in an atmosphere of attentiveness and mutual respect
before a sexual encounter can be lived truthfully again.
Illnesses, tiredness and psychological distress can also make
marital continence necessary. This will actually enhance the
truthfulness of the relationship and hence also its fruitfulness. Moreover the couple can thereby preserve ' ... the

spiritual growth that will keep the inherent power of sexuality alive and active'.[6]

Every act of communication on the sexual level has a deep impact, it cannot be undone and it leaves its mark. For when someone unites with another person, he/she becomes one with that other person (cf. 1 Co 6:14–18). This aspect of sexual intercourse is commonly overlooked or simply not taken seriously. But that is exactly why a 'fleeting or superficial relationship' is so damaging, for it reduces the most intense form of communication to something empty and banal, robbing it of its real content. This is the real problem with sexual activity outside marriage.

Sexual activity in marriage, which is grounded and lived in the truth of the partnership, is not only about union and hence about the fulfilment of the human yearning for acceptance and security; it also has to do with a kind of self-transcendence (ecstasy) which seeks not one's own satisfaction but the happiness and well-being of the other. This happiness will entail a quest for fruitfulness; though not limited to reproduction, this kind of fruitfulness finds its highest expression in that.

The fact that marriage is ordered to the mutual good of the couple underlines the human, person-centred, and sexual dimension of the union which the couple contract in the sight of God. It allows neither exaggerated individualism nor a self-sufficient egoism in the spouses, but presupposes that they have an openness to each other and to others.

The decision to love, respect, and honour another person is a decision that must be motivated by reason and guided by the will. The feeling of love on its own is simply not sufficient, 'it has to be purified, it has to undergo a process of discernment, that is, reason and will have to come into it. Reason, sentiment and will have to come together.'[7] In no way can a commitment of this kind be called irrational, for

Loving, it corresponds to the deep human desire
respecting for security and love.
and honoring Such a decision must be repeated daily,
the other confirmed, and renewed. It is about *want-*
ing to love, respect, and honour the other person. This act
of the will needs to be renewed in good and bad times alike,
in health and in sickness and also in joy and fulfilment.
Now and again love is confused with a feeling, and when
that fades, it brings an end to the relationship, since its
foundation in feeling seems to have evaporated. But the
decision to commit to marriage needs to be approached like
every other decision, since it too requires knowledge ac-
quired through reason and affirmation by the will.

Before the reception of the sacrament of marriage, it is
therefore necessary to put aside all those bad tendencies,
attitudes, and sins that can be so damaging. Only then will
grace be able to make its presence felt. This inevitably
requires a path that passes through repeated conversions—
which are manifested concretely in the sacrament of confession. Confession needs to be a part of marriage preparation—which is after all a new beginning. What is at stake is
the need for liberation from egoism and individualism,
along with any other obstacles that can be brought together
under the overarching concept of 'sin'. Sin here means the
disturbance of the original order, the order which is to be
restored in marriage; marriage being the only way that the
power of the sacrament can become operative. In general
then, it is a good thing if before the reception of the
sacrament a 'whole life confession is made'. This involves a
survey of a person's entire life, brought before God and
made the object of a review in the presence of the priest, so
that all those sins are set aside which find expression in the
words 'I will not'. Then the partners will be free to say the
great 'I will'. This means that they take as their model God's

love for humanity and put their trust in his grace and his help, help which will be pledged to them in the sacrament of marriage. In this way they create the basis for their journey together in love, respect, and honour.

FOR FURTHER REFLECTION

- *Do I see love purely or mainly as a feeling or emotion?*
- *What do respect and honour mean for our relationship?*
- *What role does sexuality play in my life?*
- *Do I want my partner for his/her own sake?*
- *What can continence in marriage mean?*
- *Am I 'right' with God, with my partner?*

Notes

1   GS 48.
2   *Ibid.*
3   CSDC 223.
4   FC 11.
5   Cf. Benedict XVI, Encyclical, *Deus caritas est*, 6–8.
6   Isabelle and Alain de Layre, 'Marriage, a Sacrament for the Road', in: Aldegonde Brenninkmeijer-Wehrhahn/Klaus Demmer (eds.), *Close to our Hearts. Personal Reflections on Marriage*, Vienna/Berlin 2013, 89.
7   Benedict XVI, *Address on the Evening of Witness*, Bresso Park, 2 June 2012.

6. WE ARE READY TO ACCEPT THE CHILDREN THAT GOD MAY SEND US

Every Christian marriage should be **Fruitfulness** fruitful, but fruitfulness must be **means: a** understood in a broader context as **fundamental** the fruit of love. The person who truly loves **acceptance of** does not shut himself up in himself, but **life** gives himself. This giving can be expressed in different ways, it involves our relationship with God as much as our relationship with our neighbour. An important part of married love and its fruitfulness is therefore the readiness to give life to children and the desire to bring them up in a Christian way. This issue is an integral part of the Christian understanding of marriage. In giving life to others, married love demonstrates its own fruitfulness and the couple open themselves to the future and become co-workers in God's creation.

This fruitfulness proper to marriage assumes a fundamental acceptance of life on the part of the couple. They declare that they are ready to accept the children whom God wants to send them for the children's own sakes. They accept children as a gift from God, in the knowledge that God has already accepted their child beforehand and loved it from all eternity. Children thus become the marvellous fruit of their love, unity, and mutual devotion.

With regard to the question of having children, two extremes need to be avoided. On the one hand, thinking of

children as an obstacle on the path to one's own self-fulfilment and hence excluding the possibility of having them
from the start. On the other hand, wanting to have children
'at any price', but not for their own sake, rather as a means
for the satisfaction of one's own needs. For:

> The desire to be a mother or a father does not justify
> any "right to children", whereas the rights of the
> unborn child are evident. The unborn child must be
> guaranteed the best possible conditions of existence
> through the stability of a family founded on mar-
> riage, through the complementarities of the two
> persons, father and mother.[1]

In a society in which boundaries are increasingly becoming
blurred because (almost) everything is seen as having the same
value, these opposite attitudes are often not really looked on
as extreme. It is necessary then for the spouses to altercate and
discuss in advance what openness to life means for them.

If a child is thought of as an obstacle on the way to
self-fulfilment, that can lead either to a fundamental rejection of the new life, or to an only very limited acceptance of
the offspring, in that only healthy children or a limited
number of children will be accepted. In his Encyclical
Humanae vitae Pope Paul VI took a stand on this.[2] Reac-
tions to this Encyclical still diverge strongly even after 50
years. Pope Francis designated it as 'prophetic' in an interview and praised the courage of his predecessor in standing
against the majority and putting on a 'cultural brake'.[3]

What was really in the mind of the then Pope? In the
1960s technology was in the ascendancy; it made everything
seem possible, and whatever it could do had to be done.
Paul VI recognised how this development was alienating
man from himself and from God, above all where man
himself became the object of technological manipulation.
He saw that the quest to subject the sexual act of married

persons to this kind of technological mentality would damage the marital relationship.[4] Contraception can easily become an expression of this mentality if it shapes the most intimate language of love. This language then gets distorted because loving union is separated from fruitfulness, so that an essential aspect of mutual self-giving is absent.

Much more damaging than contraception, however, is the effect of abortion. The situation of a married couple in their life together can prove to be complicated, unpleasant and even to some degree 'hopeless' as a result of an unexpected pregnancy. Nonetheless, abortion is never an option and not simply because the after effects (e.g. Post-abortion Syndrome) are gravely damaging, but because it involves the taking of an unborn human life. Since the first centuries of her existence the Church has designated such acts as morally reprehensible and as a serious violation of the moral law.[5] She is convinced that by the act of abortion and by direct participation in it,[6] a person puts herself/himself outside the community of the Church.[7]

Unfortunately, in today's society at large abortion is widely regarded—and indeed even promoted—as a means for the regulation of births if not propagated as a 'human right'. New forms of prenatal diagnostics further increase social pressure on married couples, and yet the consequences of abortion or of medications for abortion should not be underestimated. This 'option' should be excluded in advance.

The other extreme consists in wanting children 'at any price'. To meet this urge, there are various options open that are subject to the *diktat* of technology. Nowadays there are a great number of so-called 'Fertility Clinics', promising to provide the answer to the unfulfilled desire for children. Generally speaking, artificial fertilisation forms the basis for all the methods. As the word itself indicates, we are talking about 'artificial' intervention in the marital act, which is thereby not only robbed of its dignity but replaced by technology.[8] So the child does not have its origin in an act which arises from the mutual self-giving of the parents, but owes its being to the work of doctors and laboratory workers in the sterile environment of a clinic.

Artificial fertilisation almost always involves the selection of genetic material or embryos, especially so where pre-implantation genetic diagnosis is concerned.[9] The consequence is that in the first part of his life the person is reduced to the level of mere laboratory material. Quite apart from the effects of this mentality on the married couple's life together, it represents serious discrimination and a violation of human dignity.[10] Artificial fertilisation can moreover turn into an ordeal so devastating that it destroys a marriage.[11]

It is essential therefore that the partners discuss this whole issue before they get married, preparing themselves for the fertility that goes with marriage and for responsible parenthood. This is all the more important in that the arrival of children always presents its own **Preparing for** great challenges. If the parents are to rise to **responsible** these challenges, they have to understand **parenthood** this question within all the wider perspectives of fertility, otherwise the arrival of children may overwhelm them.

Fertility in the broadest sense is connected with the good of the married couple, but in the same way also with children, who—if 'God sends them'—are an essential element in it. So a readiness to accept the children whom God sends to the married couple is a fruit of this same fertility. On this point, the Second Vatican Council states that the married couple must

> fulfil their task with human and Christian responsibility [...] Let them thoughtfully take into account both their own welfare and that of their children,

those already born and those which the future may bring. For this accounting they need to reckon with both the material and the spiritual conditions of the times as well as of their state in life. Finally, they should consult the interests of the family group, of temporal society, and of the Church herself.[12]

If, according to this way of thinking, a married couple make up their minds to give life to a large number of children, this will represent an enrichment for Church and society and it merits not simply acknowledgement, but actual positive support and respect. Pope Francis encourages this:

> If a family with many children is looked upon as a weight, something is wrong! The child's generation must be responsible ... but having many children cannot automatically be an irresponsible choice. Not to have children is a selfish choice. Life is rejuvenated and acquires energy by multiplying: it is enriched, not impoverished![13]

Marriage is an adventure, the couple does need to learn its fundamental principles in the area of fertility. If a marriage is 'fertile', everyone benefits from that, as the Council document and Pope Francis emphasise. For one thing, it is a source of joy to the family, which thereby will become a nucleus of society and make a real contribution to its upbuilding. At the same time, it is also of fundamental significance for the Church, conferring fertility on her as well. When families, children, young people and adults are present in the life of a parish, that parish has a strong base. Fertility then has to do with a sense of responsibility, and a great deal hangs upon it.

This brings us to another point, described by the Second Vatican Council in this way: 'But in their manner of acting, spouses should be aware that they cannot proceed arbitrarily, but must always be governed according to a conscience dutifully conformed to the divine law itself, and should be submissive towards the Church's teaching office, which authentically interprets that law in the light of the Gospel.'[14]

Arbitrariness in a married couple is expressed not just by a fundamental rejection of children, avoidance of children, or abortion of children, but also in the resort to modern medicine to create 'superchildren', devoid of any connection whatsoever between loving union and procreation. Pope Francis passes a severe judgement on this 'throwaway' culture and calls for a new lifestyle.[15] Guidance in this can be found in the Magisterium of the Church, 'for the magisterium ensures our contact with the primordial source and thus provides the certainty of attaining to the word of Christ in all its integrity.'[16]

Against this background it is important for the couple to take stock at regular intervals, consult their consciences, and seek God and His will together. Fertility in marriage thus embraces a living relationship with God along with a readiness to keep working at one's marriage—and in so doing, to establish control over oneself. Only a person who respects the dignity of the other can be fruitful together with the other. This respect is expressed in the small things, for love is shown in the details.

Pope Francis summarises these small things in the three words 'please', 'thank you' and 'sorry'. These simple words and the everyday gestures corresponding to them

> hold much power: the power to keep home life intact even when tested with a thousand problems. But if they are absent, little holes can start to crack open and the whole thing may even collapse.[17]

All this calls for a culture of conversation and openness between the spouses, and that must also include the question of children. The spouses may come to the decision together that it is better at the beginning of the marriage (or

at a particular point in time) not to have **A culture of**
children, because they don't (yet) have the **conversation**
requirements needed for their care or their **and openness**
education. However, a fundamental No, **within**
the complete exclusion of fertility, would **marriage**
on the other hand completely contradict the Christian
understanding of marriage. Admittedly it may happen that
for example a wife is physically or psychologically not strong
enough to have further children without her life being put
in danger. In this kind of case there has to be respect for
such personal limitations, but not—as we have already
said—to the extent of there being a fundamental No to life.

Fertility does however need to be understood in its
broader sense, for it is not simply about having children. '…
it is enlarged and enriched by all those fruits of moral,
spiritual and supernatural life which the father and mother
are called to hand on to their children, and through the
children to the Church and to the world.'[18] So fertility
involves not just having children, but also guiding them on
their way to a fulfilled life. The Council speaks of 'spiritual
and supernatural fruits'. Children are a great good, and it is
essential, especially in today's secularised society, to give
them a solid foundation. This not infrequently means
swimming against the tide of the *Zeitgeist* [spirit of the
times] so as to live the newness of the gospel as fully as
possible.[19] If this does not happen, entry to supernatural life
remains blocked—whereas that is actually the real purpose
of life and of fertility.

If their marriage remains childless against their wish,
Christian couples can find other ways of making their love
fruitful, e.g. as foster parents, through adoption, through
involvement with (young and old) persons on the margins
of society, or in various other ways. There is huge scope
here, especially for activity in the moral and religious areas.

At their wedding, the couple will not only be asked about their readiness to accept children as a gift from God, but also whether they are ready 'to bring them up according to the law of Christ and his Church'. This task of education 'is rooted in the primary vocation of married couples to participate in God's creative activity: by begetting in love and for love a new person who has within himself or herself the vocation to growth and development, parents by that very fact take on the task of helping that person effectively to live a fully human life.'[20]

Education is a right and a duty For Christian couples, education is a right and a duty. It is a proper part of the parental role and it cannot be taken away from them under normal circumstances, nor should they fully delegate it. On this the Charter of the Rights of Families states:

> Parents have the right to educate their children in conformity with their moral and religious convictions, taking into account the cultural traditions of the family which favour the good and the dignity of the child; they should also receive from society the necessary aid and assistance to perform their educational role.[21]

The parents are free to choose appropriate means and supports to help them to carry out their educational task. They can choose from Church and state institutions (kindergarten, school, etc) the ones that correspond most closely to the Christian educational model and from which they anticipate receiving the greatest possible support. The **Christian education is all-embracing and integral** responsibility, however, remains theirs. This raises the question whether placing children in all-day nurseries can adequately fulfil this responsibility, since they cannot replace the parents and their personal care. Christian education, which is entrusted to the couple as parents, is to be understood as an all-embracing integral education, which means striving for the harmonious unfolding of the physical, spiritual, and moral aptitudes of the child: its goal is that of an all-embracing formation with a view to the mental-spiritual and social dimension of the person.

It is not enough to give children every conceivable material thing they might want, and indeed this can be counter-productive, since it all too often goes along with neglect of the other dimensions. It is quite common for extremely busy parents to use it as a way of compensating for their absence and soothing their consciences about that. The commitment, love, and security owed by parents cannot be replaced by toys and technological equipment, however expensive it may be. For education is a 'process of exchange in which the parents-educators are in turn to a certain degree educated themselves. While they are teachers of humanity for their own children, they learn humanity from them.'[22]

The social dimension of education also involves instructing children in the Christian virtues. It is fundamental that we learn what generosity, readiness for forgiveness, love of neighbour, helpfulness, renunciation, harmony, etc mean for our own lives. Children should, in accordance with what is said during baptism, open themselves to receive God's word and declare their faith to the benefit of others and to the glory of God. In the family children not only have their first experience of a life shared with others, they also acquire their first experiences of lived faith, their first experiences of the Church. So Christian education embraces not only education in responsible behaviour and in the right use of freedom, it is also education in faith and prayer, a guide to life under the Word and the call of God. In this context the significance of praying together becomes even clearer.

In this all-embracing sense, Christian education is a qualification for active participation in life in Church and society and life as an adult Christian and a citizen aware of his responsibilities.

FOR FURTHER REFLECTION

- *Do I have any desire to be a father or a mother?*
- *Am I willing to accept children for their own sake as a gift from God?*
- *Am I ready and in a position to bring up/educate children?*
- *What does the fruitfulness of marriage mean to me?*
- *Could I cope with childlessness?*

Notes

1   CSDC 235; cf. CCC 2378.

2   Cf. Paul VI, Encyclical *Humanae vitae.*

3   Cf. Interview with *Corriere della Sera* of 5 March 2014, in: *Papa Francesco, Intervista e conversazioni con i giornalisti. Due anni di Pontificato*, ed. Giuseppe Costa, Città del Vaticano 2015, 131–132.

4   Cf. HV 17.

5   Cf. CCC 2271.

6   Cf. EV 74.

7   Cf. CIC 1398.

8   For an ethical evaluation of the different methods cf. Congregation for the Doctrine of the Faith, Instruction *Donum vitae.*

9   Cf. Ralph Weimann, *Bioethik in einer säkularisierten Gesellschaft. Ethische Probleme der PID*, Paderborn, 2015.

10   Cf. Congregation for the Doctrine of the Faith, Instruction *Dignitas personae.*

11   Cf. Manfred Spieker, *Sozialethische Probleme des Lebensschutzes*, in Manfred Spieker (ed.), *Biopolitik. Probleme des Lebensschutzes in der Demokratie*, Paderborn 2009, 23–38, here 37.

12   GS 50.

13   Francis *On the Family*, San Francisco 2015, 26.

14   GS 50.

15   Cf. LS 16.

16   LF 36.

17   Francis, *On the Family*, San Francisco 2015, 64.

18   FC 28.

19   Cf. Francis, Apostolic Exhortation *Evangelii gaudium*, 259.

20   FC 36.

21   Charter of the Rights of Families, Art. 5a.

22   John Paul II, *Letter to Families*, 16.

7. I PROMISE TO BE FAITHFUL TILL DEATH US DO PART

Let us grow old together, wrote someone on the pillar of a railway bridge, and next to it a heart had been drawn with the inscription 'G + M—for ever'. Love wants lastingness, love wants 'for ever', love should never end. Typical modern signs of this desire are the love locks you can see on bridges: bearing the initials of the lovers, their keys have been thrown into the river. The expression of a desire—and sometimes also of a reality.

In the sacrament of marriage, the hearts of two persons who love one another are united, with the help of God, in an indissoluble unit. So married life means—as the Synod Fathers emphasise—not simply that the two stay together forever, but that they also love each other forever.[1] A person who takes another in the sacrament of marriage so as to found a real community for all of life can do so only without reservations. This means that any precondition, whether with respect to the relationship (union), or with respect to temporal limitation (indissolubility) would make the foundation invalid. Or, in the words of St John Paul II:

> The indissolubility of marriage, which today seems no longer comprehensible to many, is equally an expression of the unconditional dignity of man. You cannot live only on trial; you cannot die only on

trial. You cannot love just for an experiment, or accept another person temporarily and on trial.[2]

The decision to get married means: committing oneself and excluding other options

Therefore, making the decision to get married means committing oneself once and for all and excluding other options.

The image of marriage is used in the Old Testament to describe the covenant of God with His people. This symbolic union carries the further implication of a claim on the married couple: as God remains true to His people in all the changes of life, so they are called to be faithful to each other and to stand by each other whatever their life together entails. Furthermore, in the New Testament writings, marriage becomes a symbol of the unity between Christ and the Church. It becomes a sacrament, a sign of the presence of God among men, as expressed in the words of the solemn nuptial blessing:

> O God, who, to reveal the great design you formed in your love, willed that the love of the spouses for each other should foreshadow the covenant you graciously made with your people, so that, by fulfilment of the sacramental sign, the mystical marriage of Christ with his Church might become manifest in the union of husband and wife among your faithful ...

Faithfulness in marriage is especially important in times of crisis, as Robert Spaemann emphasises. The person able to fall back on a memory of 'what it is like for there to be harmony in the world' will be able to deal more easily with 'a world in which there is discord'.[3]

The mutual faithfulness of the married couple as modelled on the faithfulness of God is mentioned at several points in the wedding service. Before the couple confer the sacrament of marriage on each other, they will be asked: 'Are you ready to love and honour each other as man and wife for the rest of your lives?', while a little later they promise each other 'I do take thee ... to have and to hold from this day forward, for better or worse, for richer or poorer, to love and to cherish, till death us do part.' The celebrant says at the affirmation of the marital union 'God, the Lord, has joined you together as man and wife. He is faithful. He will be close to you and will complete the good work which he has begun in you.' 'You have declared your consent before the Church. May the Lord in his goodness strengthen your consent and fill you both with his blessings.' He concludes with the words of Scripture: 'What God has joined together, let no man put asunder' (Mt 19:6).

In regard to faithfulness in marriage, three distinctions need to be made. First of **Faithfulness** all, there is faithfulness to the marriage, **to marriage** namely the commitment of the spouses to living their partnership, to keeping faith with each other in good and in bad times until death parts them. This is not just a matter of defending the marriage covenant, it is also about consolidating and strengthening the marriage. This is something that calls for constant effort. Married couples need to look regularly together at how things stand with regard to their loyalty to their lifelong commitment to 'marriage'. The fact that the vow to be faithful is made publicly at the start of the marriage gives it a special significance, going way beyond that of a purely private promise.

The next thing to mention is faithfulness to one's spouse. It mirrors the mutual giving **Faithfulness** and receiving of self. A person makes a fully **to one's** conscious decision to commit to the one **spouse** partner, thereby excluding all others, including potential ones in the future. Nevertheless, faithfulness of this kind needs constant affirmation; it needs to prove itself, and this is not just a matter of 'physical faithfulness'. Actually it is not adultery that most damages marital faithfulness, but the fact that other persons or things in life acquire a meaning which one's own spouse does not (any longer) have. There are a thousand forms of unfaithfulness.

> There doesn't always have to be a third person, it can just as well be work, profession, anxiety, even children, even convictions and ideals. The best and the noblest, the worst and the silliest can so distract our minds and our feelings that because of them we no longer notice the other, or else we see the other only as if they are the other side of a screen or an abyss.[4]

Faithfulness to one's spouse means giving the spouse priority. If, for example, a person shares his deepest thoughts and feelings on the social networks but is not willing to share them with his spouse, faithfulness is in danger. If a person's heart becomes too focussed on something else, a marriage is in danger of collapse (cf. Mt 5:28). How important it is then to keep watch over one's heart and one's thoughts. Promising faithfulness to a person means making a verbal pledge to stand by that person. Faithfulness is very much about reliability and dependability.

Faithfulness to oneself   Finally, we should mention faithfulness to oneself, to one's own history, to one's own potential, to the truth of one's own life and one's own commitment. The necessary requirements for a person to be able to remain properly faithful to a life commitment need to be regularly pondered and reaffirmed. This is connected with the acceptance of oneself which we spoke about earlier, and it assumes that every now and then a person will pause to reaffirm his commitment. For promising to be faithful in marriage is about linking one's own life journey irrevocably with that of another person and shaping one's future in tandem with that other person.

The vow of faithfulness involves quite a risk, and it may actually seem overwhelming to the spouses, since it is connected with something unforeseeable—human beings are by nature an eternal mystery. They are always liable to change, their lives go through highs and lows, and yet the obligations of the partners with respect to the promise of faithfulness are in no way dependent on circumstances. The promise of faithfulness does not set the story of the spouses in aspic, but a person who promises faithfulness to another is saying to that other: whatever happens, I will be by your side.

By raising it to the dignity of a sacrament, the Church aims to support faithfulness in marriage with those protective frameworks and divine aids which can provide a springboard for the spouses to take this leap of faith together. But here the relationship with God is of fundamental importance, and the person who has learned to keep faithful to God will find it easier to keep faithful to a spouse. So where marital faithfulness is concerned, awareness of standing 'before God' is not something secondary, but something absolutely primary.

Lifelong faithfulness and the indissolubility of marriage are to be understood 'not as an oppressive demand, but an existential task full of promise, a task at which one works for a whole lifetime.'[5] They are a gift from God that calls for active collaboration on the part of the couple.

FOR FURTHER REFLECTION

- *Does the promise of faithfulness in marriage make me anxious, or is it an inspiration for me?*
- *Have I been/am I faithful (to myself) in my life?*
- *What does it really mean to me to be faithful to my spouse?*
- *Where does unfaithfulness begin for me?*
- *What are we making of our shared marriage enterprise?*
- *What steps do we need to take in the near future to do more justice to our vow of faithfulness?*

Notes

1   Cf. AL 123.
2   John Paul II, *Homily in Cologne*, 15 November 1980 [My translation, no official English version located].
3   Cf. Robert Spaemann, *Basic Moral Concepts*, London/New York 1991, 23.
4   Görres, *Von Ehe und von Einsamkeit*, 46.
5   Klaus Demmer, 'Sacramental Marriage—a Testimony of Faith in a Secular World', in: Aldegonde Brenningkmeijer Werhahn/Klaus Demmer (eds.), *Close to our Hearts. Personal Reflections on Marriage*, Vienna/Berlin 2013, 15.

CONCLUDING
REFLECTIONS

The subject of this book is summed up in the title *The Path to Marriage. Daring to say 'I will'*. Marriage is a joint enterprise and a risky one, for the decision to get married and the commitment to a particular partner is not easy, and neither is it something that can be taken for granted. However, if the two partners do stay on their path and overcome the obstacles that face them together, marriage will develop into a great treasure for them and life itself will become a treasure hunt, for it will bring out the very best in each other. There are so many events in life that cannot be subjected to planning or even to anticipation—and sometimes that is actually all the better. Nevertheless we can at least try to limit the risky elements and find ways of developing those positive attributes which spouses bring with them into their marriage. This book aims to draw attention to such factors. Those about to be married should not focus on their fear of failure but on a happy anticipation of life together, and this happy anticipation becomes reality in the marriage union, which Scott Hahn characterises in the simple but pregnant words 'I am yours, and you are mine'.[1]

Marriage assumes a lifelong commitment and finds expression supremely in the 'I will', which should be set upon a solid foundation (cf. Mt 7:24). The greatest enemy of every relationship is egoism, which is often further reinforced by indi-

The greatest enemy of every relationship is egoism

vidualism and by social means of communication. A person who declares that he is ready to commit to marriage must bring with him a basic willingness to say a clear 'I will not' to egoism, so as to be able to say 'I will' to himself and to the other. This is the only way to give a home to the other where the other's strengths and weaknesses are accepted and the two can set out on their path together. To love, respect, and honour the other in good days and in bad, in health and in sickness assumes values and virtues which need to be practised and fostered together. On the human level they form the spine of the relationship and they should be thoroughly tested before the wedding.

The mutual giving and accepting which finds expression in the 'I will' of marriage assumes a mature and free commitment to marry. Marriage is all about the unconditional acceptance of the other, so it must not be turned into a means for getting something else. The path followed by the spouses together has its ups and its downs, and the goal will only be reached if there is a respect for the freedom of the other and a mature understanding of oneself and the other. Nobody therefore should 'slide' thoughtlessly into marriage.

Married love must not then be equated with some kind of fleeting feeling; it finds its highest form of expression in the language of love, only a part of which involves sexuality. Married love embraces respect for the other and reverence for the other's dignity. Marriage is to be lived on an equal footing and it requires a culture of conversation between the spouses. Marriage is only truthful when the spouse is taken in love, and it must at all costs not be degraded into an instrument of passion. Sexual activity continues to be a language of love in truth as long as it is at the same time an expression of devotion and mutual respect.

Mutual devotion is fruitful by its very nature, for the one who gives, receives. Fruitfulness assumes a fundamental acceptance of life by the spouses, although this does not imply that they have a right to a child. The 'I will' of the spouses will become fruitful in the 'Yes' to life. In this way the couple will become collaborators in God's work of creation, a work which becomes particularly manifest in large families.

Giving life to children brings with it the responsibility of bringing them up and passing the faith on to them, so parents have an all-inclusive role as the first educators of their children. The 'I will' then points far beyond itself, it is open to life and to the future.

For all this to work, the 'I will' of the spouses must be seen not simply as a matter of human affirmations and qualities, but as fitting into the greater 'I will' of God. The Synod Fathers made a point of stressing this aspect: it means that the lived faith of the married couple acquires a huge significance as they set out to live marriage as a calling with the help of grace. This is the way that marriage can be fruitful and the way that it can be a real sign of the love of God for humanity.[2]

In this connection it is the task of the Church to support parents and families and to refresh them on the path they take together, helping them to **The role of the Church: to support and strengthen parents and families** grow in faith and love, and helping them to become a domestic church. Through faith the relationship of the couple will acquire an added value which will make it easier for them to cope with the risky enterprise of marriage. 'Encountering Christ, letting themselves be caught up in and guided by his love, enlarges the horizons of existence, gives it a firm hope which will not disappoint. Faith is no refuge for the fainthearted, but something which enhances our lives. It makes us aware of a magnificent calling, the vocation of love. It assures us that this love is trustworthy and worth embracing, for it is based on God's faithfulness which is stronger than our every weakness.'[3]

Believing spouses trust that, as the wedding service tells us, God will fulfil what he has begun in them. They take their cue from his faithfulness and love for humanity. Their faithfulness in marriage means faithfulness to marriage, faithfulness to a spouse and faithfulness to one's self and to a life commitment once made. Every kind of unfaithfulness which spoils the relationship through sin and endangers the original plan can be healed by upright behaviour and trust in the mercifulness of God. Imperfect though it is, the love of the spouses can be purified and elevated by the presence of God. The relationship with God serves them as a compass on their journey together, and with the help of this compass they will find their way to true love.

The vow that the spouses make to each other at the wedding can be understood at a deeper level if it is lived out of faith. The words of Alfred Delp have an abiding relevance and they can serve as a key to keeping the treasure of marriage alive: 'Let us trust to life, since we do not have to live it alone—for God lives with us'.[4]

Applying this to the context of marriage: Let us dare to say *I will*, because God who created us has loved us from all eternity and redeemed us. He walks the path together with us and anticipates our activity with His grace.

Notes

1   Scott Hahn, *Swear to God. The Promise and Power of the Sacraments*, London 2004, 61.

2   Cf. AL 71; 121; 315; 320–321.

3   LF 53.

4   Alfred Delp, *Gesammelte Schriften*, Bd. 4, Frankfurt ²1985, 195 [my translation].

THE TEXT OF THE WEDDING SERVICE

These texts are for use in the context of a church service. Depending on the wishes or the situation of the individuals concerned, the wedding may take place in the context of a Nuptial Mass or with a Service of the Word.

Questions as to readiness for Christian marriage

The celebrant first asks the bridegroom:

Celebrant: N, I shall now ask you if you freely undertake the obligations of marriage, and to state that there is no legal impediment to your marriage.

Are you ready freely and without reservation to give your-selves to each other in marriage?

Bridegroom: I am

Celebrant: Are you ready to love and honour each other as man and wife for the rest of your lives?

Bridegroom: I am

The following question, which may be omitted, if for example the age of the couple makes it an issue, is directed by the Celebrant to both bride and bridegroom:

Are you ready to accept children lovingly from God and bring them up according to the law of Christ and his Church?

Bridegroom: I am

Bride: I am

The Marriage Consent

The celebrant invites the couple to declare their consent:

The Celebrant: Since it is your intention to enter into marriage, declare your consent before God and his Church.

He addresses the bridegroom:

Celebrant: A.B., will you take C.D. here present for your lawful [wedded] wife, according to the rite of our holy Mother the church?

Bridegroom: I will.

The celebrant addresses the bride:

Celebrant: C.D., will you take A.B. here present for your lawful [wedded] husband, according to the rite of our Holy Mother Church?

Bride: I will.

The celebrant then instructs them to join their right hands. The bride's hand may be placed in that of the bridegroom by her father or by a relative or friend.

The bridegroom then says after the celebrant, or reads:

The Bridegroom: I call upon these persons here present that I, A.B. do take thee C.D. to be my lawful wedded wife, to have and to hold from this day forward, for better for worse, for richer for poorer, in sickness and in health, to love and to cherish, till death us do part.

They separate their right hands momentarily, and immediately rejoin them.

Then the bride says after the celebrant, or reads:

I call upon these persons here present that I, A.B. do take thee C.D. to be my lawful wedded wife, to have and to hold from this day forward, for better for worse, for richer for poorer, in sickness and in health, to love and to cherish, till death us do part.

Celebrant: You have declared your consent before the Church. May the Lord in his Goodness strengthen your consent and fill you both with his blessings.

What God has joined together, let no man put asunder.

People: Amen.

The blessing of the rings

The celebrant blesses the rings, saying:

Celebrant:

1. May the Lord bless this ring (these rings) which you give (to each other) as the sign of your love and fidelity.

People: Amen

2. *When one or two rings are to be blessed:*

Celebrant: Lord, bless and consecrate N and N in their love for each other. May this ring (these rings) be a symbol of true faith in each other, and always remind them of their love. Through Christ Our Lord.

People: Amen

3. *To be used only when two rings are to be blessed:*

Lord, bless these rings which we bless in your name. Grant that those who wear them may always have a deep faith in each other. May they do your will and always live together in peace, good will and love. Through Christ our Lord.

People: Amen.

The couple turn to each other.

The husband places his wife's ring on her finger, saying:

N, take this ring as a sign of my love and fidelity. In the name of the Father, and of the Son, and of the Holy Spirit.

If the husband is to receive a ring, the wife places it on his finger, saying:

N, take this ring as a sign of my love and fidelity. In the name of the Father, and of the Son, and of the Holy Spirit.

GUIDE FOR FURTHER READING

Catechism of the Catholic Church[1]

Compendium of the Social Doctrine of the Catholic Church[2]

Paul VI, Encyclical *Humanae Vitae*[3]

John Paul II, Apostolic Exhortation *Familiaris Consortio*[4]

Congregation for the Doctrine of the faith, Instruction *Donum vitae*[5]

Pontifical Council for the Family, *The Truth and meaning of Human Sexuality*[6]

Pontifical Council for the Family, *Preparation for the Sacrament of Marriage* (1996)[7]

Notes

1. www.vatican.va/archive/ENG0015/_INDEX.HTM
2. www.vatican.va/roman_curia/pontifical_councils/justpeace/ documents/...
3. w2.vatican.va/.../en/encyclicals/...vi_enc_25071968_humanae-vitae.html
4. https://w2.vatican.va/content/john-paul-ii/en/apost_exhortations/...
5. www.vatican.va/roman_curia/congregations/cfaith/documents/rc_con_c...
6. www.vatican.va/roman_curia/pontifical_councils/family/documents/rc...
7. www.vatican.va/roman_curia/pontifical_councils/family/documents/rc...

Lightning Source UK Ltd.
Milton Keynes UK
UKOW01f2035200917
309579UK00001B/50/P